HEALTHY AIR FRYER PARTY

WITH LOVE BY CATHERINE B. ROBERTS

To My Family. Thank You So Much For Supporting Me.

With Love, Catherine

Table Of Contents

Introduction	10
Why You should choose Air Fryer	13
How much should you eat?	14
What is air Fryer?	16
Tips for Cooking	17
Party Snacks and Appetizers	18
51.Mini Pancakes	18
52.Crispy And Spicy Carrot Sticks	19
53.Cheese Filled Bell Peppers	20
54.Cheesy Beef Dip	21
55.Crispy Cod Nuggets	22
56.Easy Bacon Bites	23
57.Cheesy Spinach Dip	24
58.Delicious Jalapeno Poppers	25
59.Cheddar Dill Mushrooms	26
59.Mozzarella And Tomato Salad	27
60.Crispy Cauliflower Poppers	28
61.Bacon Wrapped Brie	29
62.Crab Sticks	30
63.Tomatoes Dip	31
64.Best Onion Rings	33

© **Copyright 2021 - All rights reserved.** The content contained within this book may not be reproduced, duplicated or transmitted without direct written permission from the author or the publisher. Under no circumstances will any blame or legal responsibility be held against the publisher, or author, for any damages, reparation, or monetary loss due to the information contained within this book. Either directly or indirectly.

Legal Notice: This book is copyright protected. This book is only for personal use. You cannot amend, distribute, sell, use, quote or paraphrase any part, or the content within this book, without the consent of the author or publisher.

Disclaimer Notice: Please note the information contained within this document is for educational and entertainment purposes only. All effort has been executed to present accurate, up to date, and reliable, complete information. No warranties of any kind are declared or implied. Readers acknowledge that the author is not engaging in the rendering of legal, nancial, medical or professional advice. The content within this book has been derived from various sources. Please consult a licensed professional before attempting any techniques outlined in this book. By reading this document, the reader agrees that under no circumstances is the author responsible for any losses, direct or indirect, which are incurred as a result of the use of information contained within this document, including, but not limited to, — errors, omissions, or inaccuracies.

Best Recipes Collection

65. Garlic Salmon Balls 34
66. Garlic Tomatoes 36
67. Mushroom Stew 37
68. Cheese & Onion Nuggets 39
69. Spiced Nuts 40
70. Keto French fries 41

Party Chicken Mains 43

71. Chicken Meatballs 43
72. Chicken Tikka Kebab 44
73. Crumbed Poultry Tenderloins 47
74. Delicious Chicken Nuggets 48
75. Delicious Chicken Omelet 50
76. Easy Lemon Pepper Chicken 51
77. Special Cheeseburgers 52
78. BBQ Chicken Recipe 54
79. Air Fried Chicken Tenderloin 56
80. Almond Flour Coco-Milk Battered Chicken 57
81. Chicken, Olive, And Feta Casserole 58
82. Brine Soaked Turkey 60
83. Turkey Breakfast Sausage Patties 62
84. Air Fryer Turkey Breast 64
85. Turkey Burger Cutlets 65
86. China Spicy Turkey Thighs 67

Best Recipes Collection

Red Meats for Parties — 70

- 87. Fast Steak And Mushrooms — 70
- 88. Country Fried Steak — 72
- 89. Appetizing Korean BBQ Beef — 74
- 90. Beef & Veggie Spring Rolls — 76
- 91. Beef Korma Curry — 78
- 92. Lemon Greek Beef and Vegetables — 80
- 93. Taco Bell Crunch Wraps — 82
- 94. Charred Onions With Steak Cube BBQ — 84
- 95. Beef Brisket Recipe From Texas — 85
- 96. Chimichurri Skirt Steak — 87
- 97. Air Fryer Beef Casserole — 89
- 98. Deep Fried Duck Leg Quarters — 91
- 99. Duck Rolls — 92
- 100. Herbed Duck Legs — 94
- My Secrets To Get Better Dishes and... Extra Crunchies — 97
- MEASUREMENT CONVERSION — 102

Conclusion — 103

Introduction

Are you a diabetic who loves to cook? Your dear needs to pay attention to sugar intake in his/her diet and you need a guide?

This book is specially designed for people with diabetes who want to enjoy delicious food without worrying about the consequences.

You can have a normal life and enjoy any event now!

I will show you how easy it can be to make your favorite dishes and even some new ones that are healthier than ever! You'll also learn how to read labels, what foods are safe, and which ones might not be so good for you.

There's no need to worry about feeling deprived or hungry when cooking anymore. With this cookbook, you'll never have another boring meal again!

I know how hard it can be when you have diabetes. That's why I created this air fryer cookbook for party just for diabetics or pre-diabetics like yourself! If you want to simply pay attention to your sugar intake this guide is good , too.

 With my help, eating healthy doesn't have to be difficult or boring anymore.

Air fryer cookbook for party is the perfect guide to help you make healthier and tastier meals. It includes recipes that are tailored to your specific situation and goals, with calorie and macronutrient content in mind. You'll get a wide range of nutrients, so it's more likely that you will stick to your diet. Plus, the detailed instructions make meal preparation super simple - no prior cooking experience needed!

I have been diabetic for five years now, and in this time I have learned that life goes on; it just changes. It's not the end of the world. In fact, with a few precautions I can eat anything! Every morning I wake up to exercise at least 20 minutes before eating breakfast or lunch. Exercise is key because it controls blood sugar levels while preventing future complications like heart attacks or diabetes-related blindness. So what am I going to eat? Any food from my favorite restaurant before 12 pm is okay and after 12 pm however much you want as long as its low glycemic index foods (foods that are absorbed by your body slowly). After following these guidelines for awhile my doctor said "congratulations!" This means that

The best way to prevent hunger pangs in times of unexpected fasting is a well-stocked pantry. Stock up on these items and you'll never be stuck with nothing to eat:

Pasta, rice, canned beans or chickpeas (garbanzo beans), peanut butter, whole wheat bread crusts, frozen vegetables like peas and corn that can go straight from the freezer into boiling water for an easy side dish without any prep work required. No matter how busy life gets it's important not to let your diet suffer because when we're hungry our bodies stop burning fat as efficiently which means weight loss stalls or slows down even more than before!

Pantry List

Have a number of these items on hand at any given time. Use them as main ingredients or supplemental ingredients in your meal, and for snacks too!

Best Recipes Collection

- Apple
- Raspberries
- Loganberries
- Strawberries
- Blueberries
- Wild salmon
- Haddock
- Tuna
- Swordfish
- Mackerel
- Avocados
- Dark chocolate (75% plus)
- Red onions
- Carrots
- Greek yogurt
- Oats
- Cinnamon
- Turmeric
- Leafy greens
- Garlic
- Flaxseed
- Nuts
- Olive oil
- Coconut oil
- Bell peppers
- Black coffee
- Green juice

Why You should choose Air Fryer

If you're looking for a healthier way to cook, an air fryer might be the answer.

Air fryers use hot air instead of oil and can cook everything from french fries (zero calories)to mozzarella sticks (only 8-9 calories per gram!) They can even bake things like pizza rolls or breadsticks with no added butter or oils too. You'll be able to make all your favorite fried foods in less time without any guilt.

Healthy fast food doesn't have to be hard anymore! Get this diabetic Air Fryer cookbook today and start cooking up delicious meals that will satisfy your cravings while still being healthy. This book includes recipes for snacks, appetizers, entrees, desserts and more so there's something for everyone. Plus it comes with a recipe index so you can find what you want quickly and easily.

Order this diabetic Air Fryer cookbook now on our website!

Baking and air frying are two great ways to make nutritious food quickly. Baked goods have a lot less fat than deep fried foods, so they're better for your waistline but just as delicious! The only catch is that baking takes longer than deep frying does - you'll need patience if you want healthy fast food without all the guilt. Air fryers use hot air instead of oil to cook everything from french fries (zero calories)to mozzarella sticks (only 8-9 calories per gram!) They can even bake things like pizza rolls or breadsticks with no added butter or oils too!

Air fryers are the best way to make your kitchen clean. You can put food into a bowl or pot and then cook it in an air fryer, so you do not need big pots or pans at all! Air-fryers also have no limits when cooking with these new devices. They allow anyone from appetizers like fried mozzarella sticks to main dishes like honey baked ham and desserts such as chocolate cakes! These easy recipes that help keep your body healthy will be thought of more often than before because they save time while tasting just right too.*

How much should you eat?

When contemplating portions and combinations of the food groups you will base your diet plan on, try to focus on consuming between 2000-2800 calories a day. Ask your doctor what caloric intake you should be at - adjusting it to factors like exercise level, age and how well diabetes is managed that can play a part in coming up with the perfect figure for yourself!

A well-balanced meal should include a variety of nutrients. You'll get protein, fats, and carbs at every meal if you make use of whole grains like brown rice or quinoa with vegetables such as broccoli or green beans in addition to seafood (or eggs) for your proteins. Fill out the rest of your plate by adding healthy dairy products such as yogurt and cheese that are high in calcium to help keep bones strong while following a plant based diet rich in fiber from veggies like carrots, peppers, cucumbers onion cauliflower; fruits such as berries can also be added for their benefits on heart health!

Best Recipes Collection

- ➤ - berries, peas, lentils, whole grains (nosugar), oats, quinoa.
- ➤ - broccoli, greenbeans, asparagus, peppers, carrots, cucumbers, onions, andcauliower.
- ➤ - seafood, eggs, edamame,low fat dairy and yogurt, chicken or turkey, tuna, beans, andsoy products (tofu).

By following this basic outline, you can put together a delicious meal with many varied and flavorful foods. There are also recipes in the book that will let you substitute ingredients to change dishes and your menu! For example, if there aren't any potatoes available for eggs cheese and potato dish, try substituting sweet potatoes or beets instead. Or use zucchini or butternut squash for another delicious variation on the same theme. Don't be afraid to mix things up by moving food groups around as needed!

What is air Fryer?

An air fryer is comparable to the oven in how it roasts and bakes, yet has a distinct difference. The heating elements are situated only on top of an appliance with strong support from a large fan which results in crisp food no time at all. Instead of using pot oil for frying, this unit uses heated spinning air that ensures that hot air flows evenly around your meal without any harm coming its way! It's easy to use too; just place your dinner inside some mesh or racks-- you'll end up with wonderful golden crispy crunch like when fried by the usual means but minus excess grease and fat!

Air fryers have dominated the kitchen appliance market for their ability to make fried food without all of the guilt.

The air fryer is revolutionizing how people cook, as they are doing away with dishes that could be high in fat and calories but still enjoy it just as much!

Cooking with an air fryer is a breeze. You can cook food much faster and easier than the oven or stovetop because of its small size, but it's also super easy to clean up! The heating device at the top provides hot air that moves through and around your food in no time--just like how deep frying works. This fast circulation renders crispy foods just as well without all those messy oils from typical cooking methods so cleanup is really simple too--most systems include dishwasher-safe components for some added convenience.

Tips for Cooking

Shake the basket: open the fryer and move food around while cooking in its tray, squeezing smaller foods such asFrench fries and chips. every 5-10 minutes forbetter performance. Make sure itdoesn't cling to the bowl by gently brushing with a can ofspray cooking oil like Pam or Crisco before you cook it upcrispy (no pun intended). : To preventsplattering and excessive smoke, make sure food is drybefore frying (even if you marinate it. In the same way, besure to remove the grease from the bottom of the machineregularly while preparing high-fat items such as chickenwings.

Party Snacks and Appetizers

51. Mini Pancakes

Servings: 16 Appetizers   Prep Time: 10 Min   Cooking Time: 6 Minutes

Ingredients:

2 tsp. dried parsley

Salt and Pepper to taste

3 tbsp. Butter

1 ½ cups almond flour

3 eggs

2 tsp. dried basil

Preheat the air fryer to 250 degrees F, in a small bowl, mix the ingredients together. Ensure that the mixture is smooth and well balanced. Take a pancake mold and grease it with butter. Add the batter to the mold and place it in the air fryer basket. Cook till both the sides of the pancake have browned on both sides and serve with maple syrup.

Nutrition: Calories: 96 Protein: 0.4g   Carbs: 8.7g   Fat: 7.3g

52. Crispy And Spicy Carrot Sticks

Serves: 2   Prep Time: 10 mins.   Cooking Time: 12 mins.

Ingredients

1 tablespoon of olive oil

2 teaspoons of sugar

1 large carrot, sliced into sticks

¼ teaspoon of cayenne pepper

Salt and black pepper, to taste

1 tablespoon of fresh rosemary, chopped finely

Set the Air Fryer Oven Air Fryer Oven on Air fryer to 390 degrees F for 12 minutes. Sprinkle the carrot sticks with rest of the ingredients. Place the carrot sticks on the cooking tray. Insert the cooking tray in the Air Fryer Oven when it displays "Add Food". Flip the sides when it displays "Turn Food".

Remove from the oven when cooking time is complete. Serve warm.

Nutrition: Calories: 96 Protein: 0.4g   Carbs: 8.7g   Fat: 7.3g

53. Cheese Filled Bell Peppers

Serves: 3   Prep Time: 15 mins.   Cooking Time: 12 mins.

Ingredients:

½ cup of cream cheese

1 small yellow bell pepper

½ cup of mozzarella cheese

3 teaspoons of red chili flakes

1 small red bell pepper, tops and seeds removed

1 small green bell pepper, tops and seeds removed

Set the Air Fryer Oven Air Fryer Oven on Air fryer to 325 degrees F for 12 minutes. Combine the mozzarella cheese with cream cheese and red chili flakes in a bowl. Stuff the bell peppers with this cheese mixture and return the tops. Place the cheese filled bell peppers on the cooking tray. Insert the cooking tray in the Air Fryer Oven when it displays "Add Food". Flip the sides when it displays "Turn Food". Remove from the oven when cooking time is complete. Serve warm.

Nutrition: Calories: 185   Protein: 4.7g   Carbs: 12.8g   Fat: 13.9g

54.Cheesy Beef Dip

Servings: 12   Prep Time: 10 Min   Cooking Time: 25 Minutes

Ingredients:

1 lb corned beef, diced

¾ cup mayonnaise

14 oz can sauerkraut, drained 8 oz Swiss cheese, shredded Pepper

Salt

Fit the Air Fryer Oven Air Fryer Oven oven with the rack in position, add all ingredients into the bowl and mix well and pour into the greased baking dish. Set to bake at 400 F for 30 minutes. After 5 minutes place the baking dish in the preheated oven. Serve and enjoy.

Nutrition: Calories 283 Fat 25 g Carbs 3 g Protein 12 g

55. Crispy Cod Nuggets

Serves: 4   Prep Time: 15 mins.   Cooking Time: 10 mins.

Ingredients:

2 eggs

¾ cup of breadcrumbs

A pinch of salt

1 cup of all-purpose flour

1 pound of cod, cut into 1x2½-inch strips

2 tablespoons of olive oil

Set the Air Fryer Oven Air Fryer Oven on Air fryer to 390 degrees F for 10 minutes. Strain the flour in a shallow dish and whip the eggs in another dish. Combine the breadcrumbs with salt and olive oil in a third shallow dish. Dredge the cod nuggets in the flour, then immerse in the eggs. Coat with the breadcrumbs and place on the cooking tray. Insert the cooking tray in the Air Fryer Oven when it displays "Add Food". Flip the sides when it displays "Turn Food". Remove from the oven when cooking time is complete. Serve warm.

Nutrition: Calories: 404 Protein: 34.6g Carbs: 12.8g   Fat: 13.9g

56. Easy Bacon Bites

Servings: 4   Prep Time: 5 Min   Cooking Time: 10 Minutes

Ingredients:

4 bacon strips, cut into small pieces

1/4 cup hot sauce

1/2 cup pork rinds, crushed

Fit the Air Fryer Oven Air Fryer Oven oven with the rack in position 2. Add bacon pieces in a bowl, add hot sauce and toss well. Add crushed pork rinds and toss until bacon pieces are well coated, transfer bacon pieces in the air fryer basket then place an air fryer basket in the baking pan. Place a baking pan on the oven rack. Set to air fry at 350 F for 10 minutes. Serve and enjoy.

Nutrition: Calories 123 Fat 10.4 g Carbs 0.3 g Protein 6.5 g

57. Cheesy Spinach Dip

Servings: 12 Prep Time: 8 Min Cooking Time: 20 Minutes

Ingredients:

3 oz frozen spinach, defrosted & chopped

1 cup sour cream

1 tsp garlic salt

2 cups cheddar cheese, shredded

8 oz cream cheese

Fit the Air Fryer Oven Air Fryer Oven oven with the rack in position, add all ingredients into the mixing bowl and mix well. Transfer mixture into the baking dish. Set to bake at 350 F for 25 minutes. After 5 minutes place the baking dish in the preheated oven. Serve and enjoy.

Nutrition: Calories 185 Fat 16.9 g Carbs 2 g Protein 7 g

58. Delicious Jalapeno Poppers

Servings: 10　　　Prep Time 5 Min　　Cooking Time: 7 Minutes

Ingredients:

10 jalapeno peppers, cut in half, remove seeds & membranes

1/2 cup cheddar cheese, shredded

4 oz cream cheese

1/4 tsp paprika

1 tsp ground cumin

1 tsp salt

Fit the Air Fryer Oven Air Fryer Oven oven with the rack in position 2, in a small bowl, mix together cream cheese, cheddar cheese, cumin, paprika, and salt. Stuff cream cheese mixture into each jalapeno half. Place stuffed jalapeno peppers in air fryer basket then place air fryer basket in baking pan, place a baking pan on the oven rack. Set to air fry at 350 F for 7 minutes. Serve and enjoy.

Nutrition: Calories 69 Fat 6.1 g Carbs 1.5 g Protein 2.5 g

59. Cheddar Dill Mushrooms

Servings: 6 Prep Time: 10 Min Cooking Time: 5 Minutes

Ingredients:

9 oz mushrooms, cut stems

6 oz mozzarella cheese, shredded

1 tbsp butter

1 tsp dried parsley

1/2 tsp salt

Fit the Air Fryer Oven Air Fryer Oven oven with the rack in position 2, add parsley, cheese, butter, and salt into the bowl and mix until well combined. Stuff cheese mixture into the mushroom caps and place in the air fryer basket then place an air fryer basket in the baking pan, place a baking pan on the oven rack. Set to air fry at 400 F for 5 minutes.

Serve and enjoy.

Nutrition: Calories 141 Fat 11.5 g Carbs 1.9 g Protein 8.5 g

59. Mozzarella And Tomato Salad

Servings: 6 Prep Time 5 Min Cooking Time: 15 Minutes

Ingredients:

1 lb. tomatoes; sliced

1 cup mozzarella; shredded

1 tbsp. ginger; grated

1 tbsp. balsamic vinegar

1 tsp. sweet paprika

1 tsp. chili powder

½ tsp. coriander, ground

In a pan that fits your air fryer, mix all the ingredients except the mozzarella, toss, introduce the pan in the air fryer and cook at 360°F for 12 minutes. Divide into bowls and serve cold as an appetizer with the mozzarella sprinkled all over.

Nutrition: Calories: 185 Fat: 8g Carbs: 4g Protein: 8g

60. Crispy Cauliflower Poppers

Serves: 4   Prep Time: 10 mins. Cooking Time: 12 mins.

Ingredients

¼ cup of golden raisins, boiled

½ cup of olive oil, divided

1 tablespoon of curry powder

¼ teaspoon of salt

1 cup of boiling water

¼ cup of toasted pine nuts

1 cauliflower head, cut into small florets

Set the Air Fryer Oven Air Fryer Oven on Air fryer to 390 degrees F for 2 minutes. Pour 1 teaspoon olive oil on the pine nuts and place on the cooking tray. Insert the cooking tray in the Air Fryer Oven when it displays "Add Food". Remove from the oven when cooking time is complete and keep aside for later use. Combine cauliflower with remaining olive oil, salt, and curry powder in a large bowl. Transfer the cauliflower mixture into the cooking tray and cook in the Air Fryer Oven oven for about 12 minutes. Stir in the pine nuts and raisins to serve.

Nutrition: Calories: 322 Protein: 3g   Carbs: 12.7g   Fat: 31.3g

61. Bacon Wrapped Brie

Servings: 8   Prep Time : 10 Min   Cooking Time: 15 Minutes

Ingredients:

1 (8-oz. round Brie

4 slices sugar-free bacon.

Place two slices of bacon to form an X. Place the third slice of bacon horizontally across the center of the X. Place the fourth slice of bacon vertically across the X. It should look like a plus sign (+on top of an X. Place the Brie in the center of the bacon Wrap the bacon around the Brie, securing with a few toothpicks. Cut a piece of parchment to fit your air fryer basket and place the bacon-wrapped Brie on top. Place inside the air fryer basket. Adjust the temperature to 400 Degrees F and set the timer for 10 minutes. When 3 minutes remain on the timer, carefully flip Brie, when cooked, bacon will be crispy and cheese will be soft and melty. To serve; cut into eight slices.

Nutrition: Calories: 116 Protein: 7g Fat: 9g Carbs: 2g

62. Crab Sticks

Serves: 4 Prep Time: 10 mins. Cooking Time: 12 mins.

Ingredients:

2 teaspoon of sesame oil Cajun seasoning, to taste

1 packet of crab sticks, shred into small pieces

Set the Air Fryer Oven Air Fryer Oven on Air fryer to 320 degrees F for 12 minutes. Sprinkle the crab sticks with Cajun seasoning and sesame oil. Place the crab sticks on the cooking tray. Insert the cooking tray in the Air Fryer Oven when it displays "Add Food". Flip the sides when it displays "Turn Food". Remove from the oven when cooking time is complete. Serve warm.

Nutrition: Calories: 91.9 Protein: 5.6g   Carbs: 8.8g   Fat: 2.41g

63. Tomatoes Dip

Servings: 6   Prep Time: 5 Min   Cooking Time: 15 Minutes

Ingredients:

12 oz. cream cheese, soft

8 oz. mozzarella cheese; grated

¼ cup basil; chopped.

¼ cup parmesan; grated

4 garlic cloves; minced

1 pint grape tomatoes; halved

2 tbsp. thyme; chopped.

½ tbsp. oregano; chopped.

1 tsp. olive oil

A pinch of salt and black pepper

Put the tomatoes in your air fryer's basket and cook them at 400°F for 15 minutes, in a blender, combine the fried tomatoes with the rest of the ingredients and pulse well. Transfer this to a ramekin, place it in the air fryer and cook at 400°F for 5 - 6 minutes more. Serve as a snack.

Nutrition: Calories: 184 Fat: 8g Carbs: 4g Protein: 8g

64. Best Onion Rings

Serves: 4   Prep Time: 10 mins. Cooking Time: 10 mins.

Ingredients:

1 cup of milk

1 egg

¾ cup of dry bread crumbs

1 large onion, cut into rings

1¼ cups of all-purpose flour

Salt, to taste

Set the Air Fryer Oven Air Fryer Oven on Air fryer to 360 degrees F for 10 minutes. Strain together salt and flour in a bowl. Cream milk and eggs in another bowl. Place the dry breadcrumbs in a third dish. Dredge the onions in the salt mixture, then dip in the creamed mixture. Coat with the breadcrumbs and place on the cooking tray and spray with coconut oil spray. Insert the cooking tray in the Air Fryer Oven when it displays "Add Food". Flip the rings when it displays "Turn Food".

Remove from the oven when cooking time is complete. Serve hot.

Nutrition: Calories: 285 Protein: 10.5g Carbs: 51.6g   Fat: 3.8g

65. Garlic Salmon Balls

Preparation Time: 6-7 minutes Cooking Time: 15 minutes Servings: 2

Ingredients:

6 ounces of tinned salmon

1 large egg

1/2 cup Edam cheese, grated

2 spring onions, diced

3 tablespoons olive oil

5 tablespoons wheat germ

½ teaspoon garlic powder

1 tablespoon dill, fresh, chopped

4 tablespoons spring onion, diced

4 tablespoons celery, diced

Preheat your air fryer to 370 Fahrenheit. In a large bowl, mix the salmon, the egg, celery, onion, dill, and garlic. Shape the mixture into golf ball size balls and roll them in the wheat germ. In a minor pan, warm olive oil over medium-low heat. Add the salmon balls and slowly flatten them. Handover them to your air fryer and cook for 10- minutes.

Nutrition: Calories: 219 Total Fat: 7.7g

Carbs: 14.8g Protein: 23.1g

66. Garlic Tomatoes

Preparation Time: 7 minutes Cooking Time: 15 minutes Servings: 4

Ingredients:

3 tablespoons of vinegar

½ teaspoon thyme, dried

4 tomatoes

1 tablespoon olive oil

Salt and black pepper to taste

1 clove of garlic, minced

Preheat your air fryer to 390 Fahrenheit. Scratch the tomatoes into halves and remove the seeds. Please place them in a big bowl and toss with oil, salt, pepper, garlic, and thyme. Place them into the air fryer and cook for 15-minutes. Drizzle with vinegar and serve.

Nutrition: Calories: 28.9 Total Fat: 2.4g Carbs: 2.0g Protein: 0.4g

67. Mushroom Stew

Preparation Time: 7 minutes

Cooking Time: 1 hour and 22 minutes Servings: 6

Ingredients:

1 lb. Of chicken, cubed, boneless, skinless

2 tablespoons of canola oil

1 lb. Fresh mushrooms, sliced

1 tablespoon thyme, dried

2 tablespoons tomato paste

3 large tomatoes, chopped

4 cloves garlic, minced

¾ cup of water

1 cup green peppers, sliced

3 cups of zucchini, diced

1 large onion, diced

1 tablespoon basil

1 tablespoon marjoram

1 tablespoon oregano

Cut the chicken into cubes. Position them in the air fryer basket and pour olive oil over them. Add mushrooms, zucchini, onion, and green pepper. Mix and add in garlic, cook for 2-minutes, then add in tomato paste, water, and seasonings. Lock the air fryer and cook the stew for 50-minutes. Set the heat to 340 Fahrenheit and cook for an additional 20-minutes. Remove from air fryer and transfer into a large pan. Empty in a bit of water and simmer for 10-minutes.

Nutrition:

Calories: 53 Total Fat: 3.3g Carbs: 4.9g Protein: 2.3g

68. Cheese & Onion Nuggets

Preparation Time: 7 minutes Cooking Time: 12 minutes Servings: 4

Ingredients:

1 egg, beaten

1 tablespoon coconut oil

1 tablespoon thyme, dried

Salt and pepper to taste

Mix the onion, cheese, coconut oil, salt, pepper, thyme in a bowl. Make 8 small balls and place the cheese in the center. Place in the fridge for about an hour. With a pastry brush, carefully brush beaten egg over the nuggets. Cook for 12-minutes in the air fryer at 350 Fahrenheit.

Nutrition: Calories: 227 Total Fat: 17.3g Carbs: 4.5g Protein: 14.2g

69. Spiced Nuts

Preparation Time: 7 minutes Cooking Time: 10 minutes Servings: 3 cups
Ingredients:

1 cup almonds

1 cup pecan halves

1 cup cashews

1 egg white, beaten

½ teaspoon cinnamon, ground Pinch of cayenne pepper

¼ teaspoon cloves

salt

Combine the egg white with spices. Preheat your air fryer to 300 Fahrenheit. Toss the nuts in the spiced mixture. Cook for 25-minutes, stirring several times throughout cooking time.

Nutrition: Calories: 88.4 Total Fat: 7.6g Carbs: 3.9g Protein: 2.5g

70. Keto French fries

Preparation Time: 7 minutes Cooking Time: 20 minutes Servings: 4

Ingredients:

1 large rutabaga, peeled, cut into spears about ¼ inch wide

Salt and pepper to taste

2 tablespoons coconut oil

½ teaspoon paprika

Preheat your air fryer to 450 Fahrenheit. Mix the oil, paprika, salt, and pepper. Pour the oil mixture over the fries, making sure all pieces are well coated. Cook in the air fryer for 20-minutes or until crispy.

Nutrition: Calories: 113 Total Fat: 7.2g Carbs: 12.5g Protein: 1.9g

Party Chicken Mains

71. Chicken Meatballs

Serving: 4 Preparation Time: 10 minutes Cooking Time: 10 minutes

Ingredients:

1-lb. ground chicken 1/3 cup panko

1 teaspoon salt

2 teaspoons chives

1/2 teaspoon garlic powder

1 teaspoon thyme

1 egg

Toss all the meatball ingredients in a bowl and mix well. Make small meatballs out this mixture and place them in the air fryer basket, press "Power Button" of Air Fry Oven and select the "Air Fry" mode. Press the time button and set the cooking time to 10 minutes. Now push the Temp button and set the temperature at 350 degrees F. Once preheated, place the air fryer basket inside and close the oven door. Serve warm.

Nutrition: Calories 453 Fat 2.4 g Carbs 18 g Protein 23.2 g

72. Chicken Tikka Kebab

Preparation Time: 10 minutes Cooking Time: 17 minutes Servings: 4

Ingredients:

1 lb. chicken thighs boneless skinless, cubed

1 tablespoon oil

2 teaspoon red chili powder mild

1/2 teaspoon ground turmeric

1/2 cup red onion, cubed

1/2 cup green bell pepper, cubed

1/2 cup red bell pepper, cubed

Lime wedges to garnish

Onion rounds to garnish For marinade:

1/2 cup yogurt Greek

3/4 tablespoon ginger, grated

3/4 tablespoon garlic, minced

1 tablespoon lime juice

1 teaspoon garam masala

1 teaspoon coriander powder

1/2 tablespoon dried fenugreek leaves

1 teaspoon salt

Preparation the marinade by mixing yogurt with all its Ingredients: in a bowl.

Fold in chicken, then mix well to coat and refrigerate for 8 hours. Add bell pepper, onions, and oil to the marinade and mix well.

Yarn the chicken, peppers, and onions on the skewers. Set the Air Fryer Basket in the Air Fryer Oven Pot Duo.

Put on the Air Fryer lid and seal it.

Hit the "Air Fry Button" and select 10 minutes of cooking time, then press "Start."

Once the Air Fryer Oven Pot Duo beeps, and remove its lid. Flip the skewers and continue Air frying for 7 minutes. Serve.

Nutrition: Calories 241 Total Fat 14.2g

Saturated Fat 3.8g Cholesterol 92mg Sodium 695mg

Total Carbohydrate 8.5g Dietary Fiber 1.6g

Total Sugars 3.9g Protein 21.8g

73. Crumbed Poultry Tenderloins

Preparation Time: 15 minutes Cooking Time: 12 minutes Servings: 1

Ingredients:

1 egg

1/2 mug dry bread crumbs

2 tbsps. Vegetable oil

8 poultry tenderloins

Adjust the air fryer temperature to 350°F.

Blend egg in a small dish. Mix bread crumbs and oil in a second bowl until the mixture becomes loosened and crumbly.

Dip each poultry tenderloin into the egg dish; get rid of any residual egg. Dip tenderloins right into the crumb mix, making sure it is uniform and covered. Lay poultry tenderloins right into the basket of the air fryer. Prepare till no longer pink in the facility, about 12 mins. An Air Fryer Oven-read thermometer inserted right into the center needs to review at least 165°F.

Nutrition: Calories: 253 Carbs: 9.8g

Protein: 26.2 fat: 11.4 g

74. Delicious Chicken Nuggets

74.Serves: 4   Prep Time: 15 mins. Cooking Time: 10 mins.

Ingredients:

1 cup of panko breadcrumbs

2 tablespoons of milk

1 egg

½ tablespoon of mustard powder

1 tablespoon of garlic powder

20-ounce of chicken breast, cut into chunks

1 cup of all-purpose flour

1 tablespoon of onion powder Salt and black pepper, to taste

Set the Air Fryer Oven Air Fryer Oven on Air fryer to 390 degrees F for 10 minutes. Lay chicken, mustard powder, onion powder, garlic powder, salt, and black pepper in a food processor. Process until smooth and form into the nuggets. Strain the flour in a bowl. Cream milk and eggs in another bowl. Place the dry breadcrumbs in a third dish. Dredge the nuggets in the flour, then dip in the creamed mixture. Coat with the breadcrumbs and place on the cooking tray. Insert the cooking tray in the Air Fryer Oven when it displays "Add Food". Flip the sides when it displays "Turn Food". Remove from the oven when cooking time is complete. Serve hot.

Nutrition: Calories: 220   Protein: 12.8g Carbs: 6g   Fat: 17.1g

75. Delicious Chicken Omelet

Serves: 8　　　　　　　　　　Prep Time: 16 mins.　Cooking Time: 16 mins.

Ingredients:

½ jalapeño pepper, seeded and chopped

1 teaspoon of butter

1 onion, chopped

¼ cup of chicken, cooked and shredded

Salt and black pepper, to taste

3 eggs

Set the Air Fryer Oven Air Fryer Oven on Air fryer to 355 degrees F for 10 minutes. Sauté onions in butter over medium heat for about 4 minutes. Stir in the chicken and jalapeño pepper. Cook for about 2 minutes and dish out in a bowl. Whip eggs with salt and black pepper in another bowl. Put the chicken mixture into the cooking tray and top with seasoned eggs. Insert the cooking tray in the Air Fryer Oven when it displays "Add Food". Remove from the oven when cooking time is complete. Serve warm.

Nutrition: Calories: 209　　　Protein: 12g　　　Carbs: 11g　　　Fat: 13g

76. Easy Lemon Pepper Chicken

Serves: 4   Prep Time: 5 mins.   Cooking Time: 30 mins.

Ingredients

1 teaspoon of table salt

4 boneless-skinless chicken breasts

1 tablespoon of lemon pepper

1 1/2 teaspoon of granulated garlic

Set the Air Fryer Oven Air Fryer Oven on Air fryer to 350 degrees F for 30 minutes. Scrub the chicken breasts with salt, granulated garlic, and lemon pepper. Place the chicken on the cooking tray. Insert the cooking tray in the Air Fryer Oven when it displays "Add Food". Flip the breasts when it displays "Turn Food". Remove from the oven when cooking time is complete. Serve warm.

Nutrition: Calories: 284 Protein: 26g   Carbs: 35g   Fat: 25g

77. Special Cheeseburgers

Servings: 4   Preparation Time: 5 minutes   Cooking Time: 15 minutes

Ingredients:

1 pound 93% lean ground beef

1 teaspoon Worcestershire sauce

1 tablespoon burger seasoning

Salt

Pepper Cooking oil

4 slices cheese Buns

In a large bowl, mix the ground beef, Worcestershire, burger seasoning, and salt and pepper to taste until well blended. Spray the air fryer basket with cooking oil. You will need only a quick sprits.

The burgers will produce oil as they cook. Shape the mixture into 4 patties. Place the burgers in the air fryer. The burgers should fit without the need to stack, but stacking is okay if necessary. Pour into the Oven rack/basket. Place the Rack on the middle-shelf of the Air Fryer Oven. Set temperature to 375°F, and set time to 8 minutes Cook for 8 minutes Open the air fryer and flip the burgers. Cook for an additional 3 to 4 minutes Check the inside of the burgers to determine if they have finished cooking. You can stick a knife or fork in the center to examine the color. Top each burger with a slice of cheese. Cook for an additional minute, or until the cheese has melted. Serve on buns with any additional toppings of your choice.

Nutrition: Calories 566 Cal Fat 39 g Carbs 30 g Protein 29 g

78. BBQ Chicken Recipe

Serving: 2
Preparation Time: 5 minutes
Cooking Time: 24minutes

Ingredients:

1 (8 ounce) container fat-free plain yogurt

2 tablespoons fresh lemon juice

2 teaspoons dried oregano

1-pound skinless, boneless chicken breast halves - cut into 1-inch pieces

1 large red onion, cut into wedges

1/2 teaspoon lemon zest

1/2 teaspoon salt

1 large green bell pepper, cut into 1 1/2-inch pieces

1/3 cup crumbled feta cheese with basil and sun-dried tomatoes

1/4 teaspoon ground black pepper

1/4 teaspoon crushed dried rosemary

In a shallow dish, mix well rosemary, pepper, salt, oregano, lemon juice, lemon zest, feta cheese, and yogurt. Add chicken and toss well to coat. Marinate in the ref for 3 hours, thread bell pepper, onion, and chicken pieces in skewers. Place on skewer rack. For 12 minutes, cook it on 360oF. Turnover skewers halfway through cooking time. If needed, cook in batches. Serve and enjoy.

Nutrition: Calories 242 Carbs 12.3g Protein 31.0g   Fat 7.5g

79. Air Fried Chicken Tenderloin

Serving: 8

Preparation Time: 5 minutes

Cooking Time: 15 minutes

Ingredients:

½ cup almond flour

1 egg, beaten

2 tablespoons coconut oil

8 chicken tenderloins

Salt and pepper to taste

Preheat the air fryer for 5 minutes Season the chicken tenderloin with salt and pepper to taste, soak in beaten eggs then dredge in almond flour. Place in the air fryer and brush with coconut oil. Cook for 15 minutes at 3750F., halfway through the cooking time, give the fryer basket a shake to cook evenly.

Nutrition: Calories 130.3 Carbs 0.7g Protein 8.7 g Fat 10.3 g

80. Almond Flour Coco-Milk Battered Chicken

Serving: 4 Preparation Time: 5 minutes Cooking Time: 30 minutes

Ingredients:

¼ cup coconut milk

½ cup almond flour

1 ½ tablespoons old bay Cajun seasoning

1 egg, beaten

4 small chicken thighs

Salt and pepper to taste

Preheat the air fryer for 5 minutes, mix the egg and coconut milk in a bowl. Soak the chicken thighs in the beaten egg mixture, in a mixing bowl, combine the almond flour, Cajun seasoning, salt and pepper.

Dredge the chicken thighs in the almond flour mixture, place in the air fryer basket. Cook for 30 minutes at 3500F. Serve Warm and Enjoy.

Nutrition: Calories 590 Carbs 3.2g Protein 32.5 g Fat 38.6g

81. Chicken, Olive, And Feta Casserole

Servings: 4 Preparation Time: 5 minutes Cooking Time: 30 minutes

Ingredients:

Chicken Casserole

1½ pounds boneless chicken thighs

Salt and pepper, to taste

2 tablespoons butter

3 ounces pesto

1¼ cups coconut cream

3 ounces' green olives

5 ounces diced feta cheese

1 clove garlic, finely chopped

For Serving:

5 ounces leafy greens

4 tablespoons coconut oil

Salt and pepper, to taste

Preheat air fryer to 350-degrees F. Spray a 6-inch soufflé dish with non-stick cooking spray; set aside, put the butter in a large saucepan. Heat the pan until the butter is melt, then sauté the chicken pieces until golden. Combine pesto and cream in a container to make the sauce. Put the chicken, olives, feta, and garlic and pesto sauce in a saucepan, mix well and Bake it for 30 minutes in air fryer or until the edges are hot and brown

Nutrition: Calories 643 Fat 56.7g Carbs: 5.7g Protein 28.5g

82. Brine Soaked Turkey

Serving: 8   Preparation Time: 10 minutes   Cooking Time: 45 minutes

Ingredients:

7 lb. bone-in, skin-on turkey breast

Brine:

1/2 cup salt 1 lemon 1/2 onion

3 cloves garlic, smashed

5 sprigs fresh thyme

3 bay leaves

Black pepper

Turkey Breast:

4 tablespoon butter, softened

1/2 teaspoon black pepper

1/2 teaspoon garlic powder

1/4 teaspoon dried thyme

1/4 teaspoon dried oregano

Mix the turkey brine ingredients in a pot and soak the turkey in the brine overnight. Next day,

remove the soaked turkey from the brine, whisk the butter, black pepper, garlic powder, oregano, and thyme. Brush the butter mixture over the turkey then place it in a baking tray. Press "Power Button" of Air Fry Oven and turn the dial to select the "Air Roast" mode. Press the time button and again turn the dial to set the cooking time to 45

minutes, now push the Temp button and rotate the dial to set the temperature at 370 degrees F. Once preheated, place the turkey baking tray in the oven and close the oven door. Slice and serve warm.

Nutrition: Calories 397 Fat 15.4 g Carbs 58.5 g Protein 7.9 g

83. Turkey Breakfast Sausage Patties

Serves 4   Prep time: 5 minutes   Cook time: 10 minutes

Ingredients:

1 tablespoon chopped fresh thyme

1 tablespoon chopped fresh sage

1¼ teaspoons salt

1 teaspoon chopped fennel seeds

¾ teaspoon smoked paprika

½ teaspoon onion powder

½ teaspoon garlic powder

⅛ teaspoon crushed red pepper flakes

⅛ teaspoon freshly ground black pepper

1 pound (454 g) 93% lean ground turkey

½ cup finely minced sweet apple (peeled)

Thoroughly combine the thyme, sage, salt, fennel seeds, paprika, onion powder, garlic powder, red pepper flakes, and black pepper in a medium bowl, add the ground turkey and apple and stir until well incorporated. Divide the mixture into 8 equal portions and shape into patties with your hands, each about ¼ inch thick and 3 inches in diameter. Place the patties in a perforated pan in a single layer, select Air Fry, set temperature to 400°F (205°C), and set time to 10 minutes. Select Start to begin preheating. Once preheated, slide the pan into the oven. Flip the patties halfway through the cooking time, when cooking is complete, the patties should be nicely browned and cooked through. Remove from the oven to a plate and serve warm.

Nutrition: Calories: 397 Protein: 27.3g Carbs: 17.8g   Fat: 26.2g

84. Air Fryer Turkey Breast

Servings: 6   Prep Time: 10 Cooking Time: 60 Minutes

Ingredients:

Pepper and salt

1 oven-ready turkey breast

Turkey seasonings of choice

Preparing the Ingredients. Preheat the Air Fryer Oven Air Fryer Oven air fryer oven to 350 degrees. Season turkey with pepper, salt, and other desired seasonings, place turkey in the Oven rack/basket. Place the Rack on the middle-shelf of the Air Fryer Oven Air Fryer Oven air fryer oven. Air Frying. Set temperature to 350°F, and set time to 60 minutes. Cook 60 minutes. The meat should be at 165 degrees when done, allow to rest 10-15 minutes before slicing. Enjoy!

Nutrition: Calories: 212; Fat: 12g; Protein:24g; Carbs 10g

85. Turkey Burger Cutlets

Ingredients:

½ lb. minced turkey

½ cup breadcrumbs

A pinch of salt to taste

¼ tsp. ginger finely chopped

1 green chili finely chopped

1 tsp. lemon juice

1 tbsp. fresh coriander leaves. Chop them finely

¼ tsp. red chili powder

½ cup of boiled peas

¼ tsp. cumin powder

¼ tsp. dried mango powder

Take a container and into it pour all the masalas, onions, green chilies, peas, coriander leaves, lemon juice, ginger and 1-2 tbsp. breadcrumbs. Add the minced turkey as well. Mix all the ingredients well. Mold the mixture into round Cutlets. Press them gently. Now roll them out carefully. Pre heat the Air Fryer Oven Air Fryer Oven oven at 250 Fahrenheit for 5 minutes. open the basket of the Fryer and arrange the Cutlets in the basket. Close it carefully. Keep the fryer at 150 degrees for around 10 or 12 minutes. In between the cooking process, turn the Cutlets over to get a uniform cook. Serve hot with mint sauce.

Nutrition: Calories: 246 Protein: 37.2g Carbs: 9.4g   Fat: 7.1g

86. China Spicy Turkey Thighs

Serves 6
Prep time: 10 minutes
Cook time: 25 minutes

Ingredients:

1 kg max turkey thighs

1 teaspoon Chinese five-spice powder

¼ teaspoon pepper

1 teaspoon salt

1 tablespoon Chinese rice vinegar

1 tablespoon mustard

1 tablespoon chili sauce

2 tablespoons soy sauce

Cooking spray

Spritz a perforated pan with cooking spray, rub the turkey thighs with five-spice powder, Sichuan pepper, and salt on a clean work surface. Put the turkey thighs in the perforated pan and spritz with cooking spray. Select Air Fry of the oven. Set temperature to 360°F (182°C) and set time to 22 minutes. Press Start to begin preheating, once preheated, place the pan into the oven. Flip the thighs at least three times during the cooking. When cooking is complete, the thighs should be well browned. Meanwhile, heat the remaining ingredients in a saucepan over medium-high heat. Cook for 3 minutes or until the sauce is thickened and reduces to two thirds. Transfer the thighs onto a plate and baste with sauce before serving.

Nutrition: Calories 274 Fat 8.3g Carbs 0.3g Protein 23.8g

Best Recipes Collection

Red Meats for Parties

87. Fast Steak And Mushrooms

Serves: 4   Prep Time: 5 mins.   Cooking Time: 14 mins.

Ingredients:

1 teaspoon of parsley flakes

1 teaspoon of paprika

1-pound beef sirloin steak, cubed

1/4 cup of Worcestershire sauce

1 tablespoon of olive oil

1 teaspoon of crushed chili flake

8-ounces of button mushrooms, sliced

Set the Air Fryer Oven Air Fryer Oven on Air fryer to 350 degrees F for 14 minutes. Combine the steak and mushrooms with olive oil, Worcestershire sauce, parsley, paprika, and chili flakes in a large bowl. Cover the bowl and marinate the steaks for about 3 hours in the refrigerator. Transfer the marinated steaks and mushrooms in the cooking tray. Insert the cooking tray in the Air Fryer Oven when it displays "Add Food". Flip the steaks when it displays "Turn Food". Remove from the oven when cooking time is complete. Serve hot.

Nutrition: Calories: 405 Protein: 45.3g Carbs: 6.1g   Fat: 22.7g

88. Country Fried Steak

Servings: 2
Preparation Time: 5 minutes
Cooking Time: 12 minutes

Ingredients:

1 tsp. pepper

2 C. almond milk

2 tbsp. almond flour

6 ounces ground sausage meat

1 tsp. pepper

1 tsp. salt

1 tsp. garlic powder

1 tsp. onion powder

1 C. panko breadcrumbs

1 C. almond flour

3 beaten eggs

6 ounces sirloin steak, pounded till thin

Season panko breadcrumbs with spices, dredge steak in flour, then egg, and then seasoned panko mixture. Place into air fryer basket, set temperature to 370°F, and set time to 12 minutes. To make sausage gravy, cook sausage and Dry outof fat, but reserve 2 tablespoons, add flour to sausage and mix until incorporated.

Gradually mix in milk over medium to high heat till it becomes thick. Season mixture with pepper and cook 3 minutes longer, serve steak topped with gravy and enjoy.

Nutrition: Calories 395 Cal Fat 11 g Carbs 0 g Protein 39 g

89. Appetizing Korean BBQ Beef

Serves: 2   Prep Time: 5 mins.   Cooking Time: 15 mins.

Ingredients:

For the meat:

1 lb. of Flank steak, sliced

1/4 cup of corn starch

Coconut oil spray

For the sauce:

1/2 cup of soy sauce

1 clove garlic crushed

1 tablespoon of hot chili sauce

1 teaspoon ground ginger

1 tablespoons of Pompeian white wine vinegar

1/2 teaspoon of sesame seeds

1/2 cup of brown sugar

1 teaspoon of cornstarch

1 teaspoon of water

Set the Air Fryer Oven Air Fryer Oven on Air fryer to 390 degrees F for 10 minutes. Dredge the steaks in the corn-starch in a large bowl. Transfer the steaks in the cooking tray and spray with coconut oil spray. Insert the cooking tray in the Air Fryer Oven when it displays "Add Food". Flip the steaks when it displays "Turn Food". Remove from the oven when cooking time is complete. Meanwhile, combine all the ingredients for sauce in another bowl except water and corn-starch. Whisk corn- starch with water and drizzle in the sauce mixture. Simmer on heat for about 5 minutes. Trickle the sauce over the steaks and serve hot.

Nutrition: Calories: 545 Protein: 42.5g Carbs: 0.7g   Fat: 36.4g

90. Beef & Veggie Spring Rolls

Servings: 10
Preparation Time: 5 minutes
Cooking Time: 12 minutes

Ingredients:

1 ounce Asian rice noodles

1 tablespoon sesame oil

7-ounce ground beef

1 small onion, chopped

3 garlic cloves, crushed

1 cup fresh mixed vegetables

1 teaspoon soy sauce

1 packet spring roll skins

2 tablespoons water

Olive oil, as required

Soak the noodles in warm water till soft, dry out and cut into small lengths. In a pan heat the oil and add the onion and garlic and sauté for about 4-5 minutes. Add beef and cook for about 4-5 minutes, add vegetables and cook for about 5-7 minutes or till cooked through. Stir in soy sauce and remove from the heat, immediately, stir in the noodles and keep aside till all the juices have been absorbed.

Preheat the Air Fryer Oven to 350 degrees F., place the spring rolls skin onto a smooth surface. Add a line of the filling diagonally across. Fold the top point over the filling and then fold in both sides, on the final point, brush it with water before rolling to seal. Brush the spring rolls with oil, arrange the rolls in batches in the air fryer and Cook for about 8 minutes. Repeat with remaining rolls. Now, place spring rolls onto a baking sheet. Bake it for about 6 minutes per side.

Nutrition: Calories 364 Cal Fat 9 g Carbs 39 g Protein 32 g

91. Beef Korma Curry

Preparation Time: 10 minutes Cooking Time: 17-20 minutes

Servings: 4

Ingredients:

1 pound (454 g) sirloin steak, sliced

½ cup yogurt

1 tablespoon curry powder

1 tablespoon olive oil

1 onion, chopped

1 cloves garlic, minced

1 tomato, diced

½ cup frozen baby peas, thawed

In a medium bowl, combine the steak, yogurt, and curry powder. Stir and set aside.

In a metal bowl, combine the olive oil, onion, and garlic. Bake at 350°F (177°C) for 3 to 4 minutes or until crisp and tender.

Add the steak along with the yogurt and the diced tomato. Bake for 12 to 13 minutes or until steak is almost tender.

Stir in the peas and bake for 2 to 3 minutes or until hot. Nutrition:

Calories: 299 Fat: 11g Protein: 38g Carbs: 9g

Fibre: 2g Sugar 3g

Sodium: 100mg

92. Lemon Greek Beef and Vegetables

Preparation Time: 10 minutes Cooking Time: 9-19 minutes Servings: 4

Ingredients:

½ pound (227 g) 96% lean ground beef

2 medium tomatoes, chopped

1 onion, chopped

1 garlic cloves, minced

2 cups fresh baby spinach

2 tablespoons freshly squeezed lemon juice

1/3 cup low-sodium beef broth

2 tablespoons crumbled low-sodium feta cheese

In a baking pan, crumble the beef. Place in the air fryer basket. Air fry at 370°F (188°C) for 3 to 7 minutes, stirring once during cooking until browned. Drain off any fat or liquid.

Swell the tomatoes, onion, and garlic to the pan. Air fry for 4 to 8 minutes more, or until the onion is tender.

Add the spinach, lemon juice, and beef broth.

Air fry for 2 to 4 minutes more, or until the spinach is wilted. Sprinkle with the feta cheese and serve immediately.

Nutrition: Calories: 98 Fat: 1g Protein: 15g Carbs: 5g

Fibre: 1g Sugar: 2g Sodium: 123mg

93. Taco Bell Crunch Wraps

Servings: 6　　Preparation Time: 10 minutes　Cooking Time: 2 minutes

Ingredients:

6 wheat tostadas

2 C. sour cream

2 C. Mexican blend cheese

2 C. shredded lettuce

12 ounces low-sodium nacho cheese

3 Roma tomatoes

6 12-inch wheat tortillas

1 1/3 C. water

2 packets low-sodium taco seasoning

2 pounds of lean ground beef

Ensure your air fryer is preheated to 400 degrees, make beef according to taco seasoning packets. Place 2/3 C. prepared beef, 4 tbsp. cheese, 1 tostada, 1/3 C. sour cream, 1/3 C. lettuce, 1/6th of tomatoes and 1/3 C. cheese on each tortilla, fold up tortillas edges and repeat with remaining ingredients. Lay the folded sides of tortillas down into the air fryer and spray with olive oil, set temperature to 400°F, and set time to 2 minutes Cook 2 minutes till browned.

Nutrition: Calories 311 Cal Fat 9 g Carbs 30 g Protein 22 g

94. Charred Onions With Steak Cube BBQ

Servings: 3   Preparation Time: 5 minutes   Cooking Time: 40 minutes

Ingredients:

1 cup red onions cut into wedges

1 tablespoon dry mustard

1 tablespoon olive oil

1-pound boneless beef sirloin, cut into cubes

Salt and pepper to taste

Preheat the air fryer to 390°F., place the grill pan accessory in the air fryer. Toss all ingredients in a bowl and mix until everything is coated with the seasonings, place on the grill pan and cook for 40 minutes. Halfway through the cooking time, give a stir to cook evenly.

Nutrition: Calories 260 Cal Fat 10.7 g Carbs 0 g Protein 35.5 g

95. Beef Brisket Recipe From Texas

Servings: 8 Preparation Time: 15 minutes Cooking Time: 1 hour and 30 minutes

Ingredients:

1 ½ cup beef stock

1 bay leaf

1 tablespoon garlic powder

1 tablespoon onion powder

1 3/4 pounds beef brisket, trimmed

2 tablespoons chili powder

2 teaspoons dry mustard

4 tablespoons olive oil

Salt and pepper to taste

Preheat the Air Fryer Oven for 5 minutes Place all ingredients in a deep baking dish that will fit in the air fryer, bake it for 1 hour and 30 minutes at 400°F. Stir the beef every after 30 minutes to soak in the sauce.

Nutrition: Calories 306 Cal Fat 24.1 g Carbs 10 g Protein 18.3 g

96. Chimichurri Skirt Steak

Servings: 2   Preparation Time: 10 minutes   Cooking Time: 8 minutes

Ingredients:

1 x 8 oz. skirt steak

1 cup finely chopped parsley

2 tbsp. fresh oregano (washed & finely chopped)

3 finely chopped cloves of garlic

¼ cup finely chopped mint

1 tsp. red pepper flakes (crushed)

1 tbsp. ground cumin

1 tsp. cayenne pepper

2 tsp. smoked paprika

1 tsp. salt

¼ tsp. pepper

¾ cup oil

3 tbsp. red wine vinegar

Throw all the ingredients in a bowl (besides the steak) and mix well, put ¼ cup of the mixture in a plastic baggie with the steak and leave in the fridge overnight (8 - 10hrs). Leave the bag out at room temperature for at least 30 min before popping into the air fryer.

Preheat for a minute or two to 390° F before cooking until med-rare (8-10 min). Pour into the Oven rack/basket. Place the Rack on the middle-shelf of the Air Fryer Oven. Set temperature to 390°F, and set time to 10 minutes, put 2 Tbsp. of the chimichurri mix on top of each steak before serving.

Nutrition: Calories 308.6 Cal Fat 22.6 g Carbs 3 g Protein 23.7 g

97 Air Fryer Beef Casserole

Servings: 4 Preparation Time: 5 minutes Cooking Time: 30 minutes

Ingredients:

1 green bell pepper, seeded and chopped

1 onion, chopped

1-pound ground beef

3 cloves of garlic, minced

3 tablespoons olive oil

6 cups eggs, beaten

Salt and pepper to taste

Preheat the Air Fryer Oven for 5 minutes, in a baking dish that will fit in the air fryer, mix the ground beef, onion, garlic, olive oil, and bell pepper. Season it with salt and pepper to taste. Pour in the beaten eggs and give a good stir, place the dish with the beef and egg mixture in the air fryer. Pour into the Oven rack/basket. Place the Rack on the middle-shelf of the Air Fryer Oven. Set temperature to 325°F, and set time to 30 minutes. Bake it for 30 minutes

Nutrition: Calories 1520 Cal Fat 15.1 g Carbs 10 g Protein 87.9 g

98. Deep Fried Duck Leg Quarters

Serves 4   Prep time: 5 minutes   Cook time: 45 minutes

Ingredients:

4 (½-pound / 227-g) skin-on duck leg quarters

2 medium garlic cloves, minced

½ teaspoon salt

½ teaspoon ground black pepper

Spritz a perforated pan with cooking spray, on a clean work surface, rub the duck leg quarters with garlic, salt, and black pepper. Arrange the leg quarters in the perforated pan and spritz with cooking spray. Select Air Fry of the oven. Set temperature to 300°F (150°C) and set time to 30 minutes. Press Start to begin preheating, once preheated, place the pan into the oven. After 30 minutes, remove the pan from the oven. Flip the leg quarters. Increase temperature to 375 F and set time to 15 minutes. Return the pan to the oven and continue cooking. When cooking is complete, the leg quarters should be well browned and crispy. Remove the duck leg quarters from the oven and allow to cool for 10 minutes before serving.

Nutrition: Calories: 235 Protein: 14g   Carbs: 34.4g   Fat: 5.5g

99. Duck Rolls

Servings: 3　　Prep Time: 10 Min　　Cooking Time: 40 Minutes

Ingredients:

1 pound duck breast fillet, each cut into 2 pieces

3 tablespoons fresh parsley, finely chopped

2 small red onion, finely chopped

1 garlic clove, crushed

1 tablespoons olive oil

1½ teaspoons ground cumin

1 teaspoon ground cinnamon

½ teaspoon red chili powder

Salt, to taste

Preheat the Air fryer to 355 degree F and grease an Air fryer basket, mix the garlic, parsley, onion, spices, and 1 tablespoon of olive oil in a bowl. Make a slit in each duck piece horizontally and coat with onion mixture, roll each duck piece tightly and transfer into the Air fryer basket. Cook for about 40 minutes and cut into desired size slices to serve.

Nutrition : Calories: 239 Fats: 8.2g Carbs: 3.2g Proteins: 37.5g

100. Herbed Duck Legs

Servings: 2   Prep Time: 5 Min   Cooking Time: 30 Minutes

Ingredients:

½ tablespoon fresh thyme, chopped

½ tablespoon fresh parsley, chopped

2 duck legs

1 garlic clove, minced

1 teaspoon five spice powder

Salt and black pepper, as required

Preheat the Air fryer to 340 degree F and grease an Air fryer basket, mix the garlic, herbs, five spice powder, salt, and black pepper in a bowl. Rub the duck legs with garlic mixture generously and arrange into the Air fryer basket. Cook for about 25 minutes and set the Air fryer to 390 degree F., cook for 5 more minutes and dish out to serve hot.

Nutrition: Calories: 138 Fat: 4.5g Carbs: 1g Protein: 25g

My Secrets To Get Better Dishes and... Extra Crunchies

Do you want to know how to get extra crunchies?

You've come to the right place. I have a few tricks up my sleeve that will make your food taste better and be healthier than ever before. These are some of my secrets for getting better dishes and more crunchies, crispies.

If you follow these tips, you can enjoy all the benefits of eating healthy without giving up any flavor or texture. And don't worry about feeling deprived because this is not a diet - it's just a way of life!

What Other Air Fryer Lovers Don't know...

- Use olive oil instead of butter in recipes

- Add spices like garlic powder or cayenne pepper to foods for an added kick

- Make sure your pan is hot enough when cooking so that the food doesn't stick and burn on the bottom

- Cook vegetables with high water content first (like onions) then add other vegetables later on in the process so they don't get too soggy from sitting in liquid too long while waiting their turn at being cooked

- When baking cookies, use parchment paper instead of greasing pans because it makes them easier to remove from the pan after baking without breaking apart into pieces which means less clean up time!

- For pancakes, use whole wheat flour instead of white flour which has been processed many times over and has lost most nutrients by now; also try adding cinnamon or vanilla extract for an even tastier dish

1. A rotisserie is a marvelous invention that can save you time in the kitchen. The only downside to this cooking tool is forgetting what's going on once it starts turning! When using a rotisserie, always put your food before touching the Start button so as not to forget anything else when everything moves around.

2. For those of us who don't enjoy the taste or texture of overcooked food, it is important to keep an eye on our cooking time. Fortunately there's a simple way to avoid this: cover your dish with foil! This will help you from over-cooking and ensure that all parts come out tender and juicy when served. Remember not get too close so as not let steam burn your skin!

3. There are many different ways to cook food, but if you don't want any hassle it's best just to oven-bake them. All the other cooking methods can be done well with an activated oven and a little patience. After activating your oven (and waiting for its temperature gauge), add some fresh ingredients - veggies or meat of choice will do nicely! Let your meal fully bake on medium heat before taking out so that every last bit is cooked through satisfactorily. But what about rotisserie chicken? Well, since all these foods need only one heating point from which they spread their flavors evenly throughout the dish, in short order there'll be nothing left not too dry up...no siree "broiling" isn't necessary either.

4. It's always a good idea to dry your foods before you start cooking them, especially in the air fryer oven. If excess steam and splatter are left unchecked for too long it can leave a mess on any nearby surfaces such as countertops or linens."

5. However… not all of the food that you cook in an air-fryer needs to be dried. But, if there is a chance it will get too wet for your liking or cause any splattering on the inside walls then by all means dry it first!

6. Spraying cooking oil on your food can help it develop a more delicious flavor. Cooks and chefs have been doing this for centuries, but you don't need to be an expert cook in order to

7. enjoy the benefits of using cooking oils as seasoning agents!

8. To make fries crispy and golden, put potatoes in cold water for 15 minutes. Dry them off, then spray with some oil before putting them into an oven that is heated to 400 degrees Fahrenheit.

MEASUREMENT CONVERSION

VOLUME EQUIVALENTS (DRY)

US STANDARD	METRIC (APPROXIMATE)
1/8 teaspoon	0.5 mL
1/4 teaspoon	1 mL
1/2 teaspoon	2 mL
3/4 teaspoon	4 mL
1 teaspoon	5 mL
1 tablespoon	15 mL
1/4 cup	59 mL
1/2 cup	118 mL
3/4 cup	177 mL
1 cup	235 mL
2 cups	475 mL
3 cups	700 mL
4 cups	1 L

VOLUME EQUIVALENTS (LIQUID)

US STANDARD	US STANDARD (OUNCES)	METRIC (APPROXIMATE)
2 tablespoons	1 fl.oz.	30 mL
1/4 cup	2 fl.oz.	60 mL
1/2 cup	4 fl.oz.	120 mL
1 cup	8 fl.oz.	240 mL
1 1/2 cup	12 fl.oz.	355 mL
2 cups or 1 pint	16 fl.oz.	475 mL
4 cups or 1 quart	32 fl.oz.	1 L
1 gallon	128 fl.oz.	4 L

TEMPERATURES EQUIVALENTS

FAHRENHEIT(F)	CELSIUS(C) (APPROXIMATE)
225 °F	107 °C
250 °F	120 °C
275 °F	135 °C
300 °F	150 °C
325 °F	160 °C
350 °F	180 °C
375 °F	190 °C
400 °F	205 °C
425 °F	220 °C
450 °F	235 °C
475 °F	245 °C
500 °F	260 °C

WEIGHT EQUIVALENTS

US STANDARD	METRIC (APPROXIMATE)
1 ounce	28 g
2 ounces	57 g
5 ounces	142 g
10 ounces	284 g
15 ounces	425 g
16 ounces (1 pound)	455 g
1.5 pounds	680 g
2 pounds	907 g

Conclusion

Diabetic Air-Fryer Cookbook cookware is not just for diabetic air fryers, it also cooks your food evenly and quickly so you can enjoy more time to talk with the people around you. It's durable and nonstick which means that after each use there will be no scrubbing needed - all of this without sacrificing quality or cleanliness when cooking; what could make a meal better?

A Diabetic Air-Fryer Cookbook air fryer is an easy way to cook healthy food, and they are great for one-hand operation. They also have a reversible stainless steel handle so you can carry it on your hip or in your hand!

There are a lot of unhealthy food options on the market today. For those with diabetes or who don't have much time, cooking is challenging because it's hard to make healthy fast foods. This Cookbook was written specifically for these people and can help them learn how to cook safely so they can enjoy their favorite dishes without risking health complications in the future.

The guide is the perfect way to ensure that you never worry about your diet again. It contains all of the recipes and instructions for how to prepare healthy meals during a fast or when suffering from diabetes.

Best Recipes Collection

It is a difficult task to cook for someone with diabetes. You would be wise not only in following the instructions carefully but also put into consideration some tips so that you can prepare healthy dishes and foods without making anyone feel like they're being deprived of flavor or restrictions on their diet.

Enjoy it!

Best Recipes Collection

Best Recipes Collection

www.ingramcontent.com/pod-product-compliance
Lightning Source LLC
Chambersburg PA
CBHW080610170426
43209CB00007B/1393